D1085267

CREATE IT!

IMPRESSIONIST ART

Alix Wood

 Gareth Stevens
PUBLISHING

Thank you to
Davina Cresswell
and Jemma Martin
for their help with
this book.

Please visit our website, **www.garethstevens.com**. For a free color catalog of all
our high-quality books, call toll free 1-800-542-2595 or fax 1-877-542-2596.

Cataloging-in-Publication Data
Names: Wood, Alix.
Title: Impressionist art / Alix Wood.
Description: New York : Gareth Stevens Publishing, 2017. | Series: Create it! | Includes index.
Identifiers: ISBN 9781482450286 (pbk.) | ISBN 9781482450309 (library bound) |
    ISBN 9781482450293 (6 pack)
Subjects: LCSH: Impressionism (Art)--Juvenile literature.
Classification: LCC ND192.I4 W66 2017| DDC 759.05'4--dc23

First Edition

Published in 2017 by
Gareth Stevens Publishing
111 East 14th Street, Suite 349
New York, NY 10003

Copyright © 2017 Alix Wood Books

Produced for Gareth Stevens by Alix Wood Books
Designed by Alix Wood
Editor: Eloise Macgregor

Photo credits: Cover, 1, 6, 7, 9, 11, 12, 14 middle and bottom, 15, 17, 18 middle and bottom, 19, 23, 24 bottom, 25, 27,
28 right, 29 © Alix Wood; 3, 14 top, 18 top, 21 © Dollar Photo Club; 5 top © Nadar; 8 © Museum of Fine Arts, Boston;
20 © Art Institute of Chicago; 22 © Metropolitan Museum of Art; 26 © Musee d'Orsay; all remaining images are in
the public domain.

All rights reserved. No part of this book may be reproduced in any form without
permission from the publisher, except by reviewer.

Printed in the United States of America
CPSIA compliance information: Batch #CS16GS: For further information contact
Gareth Stevens, New York, New York at 1-800-542-2595.

CONTENTS

What Is Impressionist Art?...............4

Claude Monet...6

Create It! – Monet.................................8

Alfred Sisley..10

Camille Pissarro.................................12

Create It! – Pissarro 14

Georges Seurat...................................16

Create It! – Seurat............................18

Gustave Caillebotte 20

Paul Cézanne 22

Create It! – Cézanne........................24

Edgar Degas..26

Create It! – Degas............................28

Glossary 30

Further Information.........................31

Index 32

WHAT IS IMPRESSIONIST ART?

Impressionist art began in France in the 1860s. A group of artists **rebelled** against the usual style of painting chosen to be shown at the famous gallery, *The Salon*. Impressionists had discovered a new style. They wanted to capture the moment, with its light and color, rather than paint fine details. **Art critics** said their work looked like "impressions" rather than paintings, and the name stuck!

This famous painting by Claude Monet, called *Impression: Sunrise*, was laughed at when it was first shown.

Meet an Impressionist Artist

Claude Monet painted some of the most well-known Impressionist paintings. He often painted the same scene several times, at different times of day. Monet and his team of gardeners created a beautiful garden at his house. He often painted his Japanese bridge and pond, below.

CLAUDE MONET

Claude Monet is probably best known for his paintings of his pond and water lilies. See if you can create an Impressionist painting of Monet's pond and bridge.

CREATE IT!

You will need: masking tape, a pencil, paper, poster paint, an eraser, a blue colored pencil

1 Draw two **arcs** on the paper using a pencil. Join them with some upright lines. Place masking tape over your drawing. Use several small pieces to gradually create the arcs.

2 Using your finger, dab on the poster paint. The painting will look best if you overlap the masking tape.

3 Once the paint is completely dry, gently peel off the masking tape. If the paper starts to rip, wait a little longer. It means your paper isn't dry enough yet.

4 Rub out any pencil lines with an eraser.

5 Now color in the bridge. You can use colored pencil, or a paintbrush and paint.

Monet's *Water Lilies* painted in 1905

TECHNIQUE TIPS

If you look at Monet's water lily painting above, can you see upside-down trees reflected in the pond? Water can act like a mirror, showing a reflection of trees and sky on its surface. That is why water usually looks blue if the sky is blue, and gray if the sky is cloudy.

CREATE IT!

You will need: a pencil, watercolor paints, pastels, paper, a paintbrush, hairspray

1 Roughly paint a pale blue sky and a line of muddy green trees.

2 Turn your paper upside down. Using pastels, draw groups of light green, oval lily leaves. Put a little dark green shadow under each one. Pastels smudge easily, so be careful.

3 Draw some white flowers. Give some groups a pink center and some a yellow center.

4 Using a dark blue or green pastel, smudge a shadow under the groups of lilies. When you have finished, ask an adult to spray your picture with hairspray to keep it from smudging.

ALFRED SISLEY

Alfred Sisley was British but lived in France for most of his life. Like most Impressionists, he liked to paint outside. He was a master at painting skies. Sisley used the direction of his brushstrokes to make his skies look full of movement.

Sisley's blustery sky in *View of Saint-Mammès*, painted around 1880

CREATE IT!

You will need: paper, crayons, watercolor paint, a paintbrush

1 Imagine a sky on a windy day. Using crayon, draw short lines in the direction the wind is blowing.

2 Now draw some trees using short lines. Have their lines blowing in the same direction

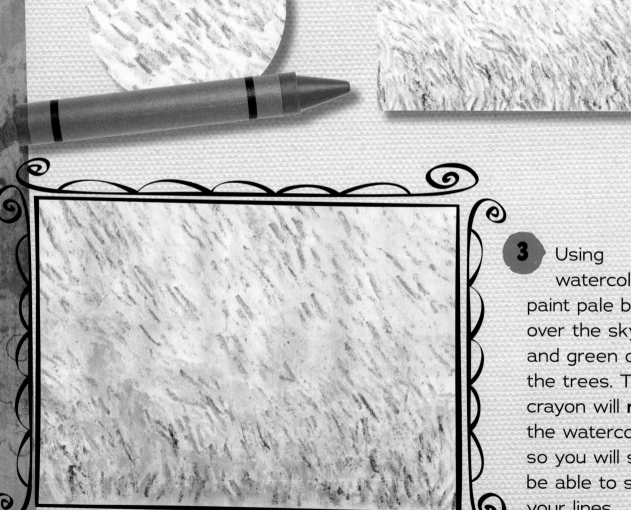

3 Using watercolor, paint pale blue over the sky and green over the trees. The crayon will **resist** the watercolor, so you will still be able to see your lines.

CAMILLE PISSARRO

Camille Pissarro liked to paint the countryside. He painted outside "**en plein air**" and often painted the changing seasons.

Pissarro's *The Orchard,* and below, a close-up of the blossom

TECHNIQUE TIPS

If you stand very close to an Impressionist painting, it often looks like just a lot of paint blobs. Only when you move farther away does the painting become recognizable. Try painting at arm's length, standing at an **easel**, like Impressionist painters would have done.

CREATE IT!

You will need: colored paper, pastels

1 Using the flat side of your pastel, shade in the sky and soil.

2 Draw gray trees. Add some patches of grass to the soil.

3 Add some shadows, and light and dark green leaves.

4 Using white pastel, draw on the blossoms. Be careful not to smudge the tree. You can add more shadows, too.

CREATE IT!

You will need: watercolor paints, paper, a paintbrush

1 Create a whole painting using obvious brushstrokes. First, find something you'd like to paint. You could use a photograph, or be like a true Impressionist and paint outside from real life.

2 Using a pencil, draw the outline of your picture on your paper. Don't add any details as you'll be painting over it.

TECHNIQUE TIPS

When you add your paint, use a small paintbrush. Make small, even marks. The marks can go in any direction you like. The most important thing is to choose the right colors for each area.

14

3 Gradually fill your paper with different colored brushstrokes. Let one color dry before you start the next color, so they don't seep into each other. When doing areas such as grass, use several different **shades** of green. Try to not leave any paper showing through.

4 Half-closing your eyes while looking at your painting helps you see what it will look like from farther away. When you have finished, walk away from your picture. See how great your painting looks from a distance!

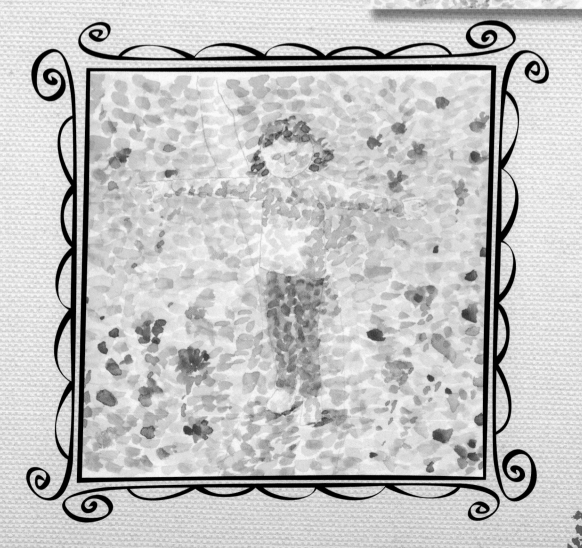

GEORGES SEURAT

French painter Georges Seurat developed a technique known as **pointillism**. He used thousands of tiny dots in **primary colors** to create his paintings. Red, yellow, and blue are primary colors. All the other paint colors can be mixed by using red, yellow, and blue. Instead of mixing his colors, though, Seurat placed dots of color next to each other.

Seurat's most famous pointillism painting
A Sunday Afternoon on the Island of La Grande Jatte

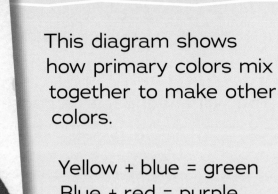

This diagram shows how primary colors mix together to make other colors.

Yellow + blue = green
Blue + red = purple
Red + yellow = orange

Try mixing some colors yourself this way.

TECHNIQUE TIPS

Instead of mixing colors, pointillism relies on the eyes and mind of the viewer to **blend** the colored dots together. By placing different colored dots next to each other, Seurat could create many colors. Hold this page a long way away. You should see green, purple, and orange circles!

CREATE IT!

You will need: paper; a pencil; red, blue, and yellow poster paint; a cotton swab

1 Draw your design on a piece of paper. It takes a long time to fill your paper with dots, so don't use a very large sheet!

2 You want all your dots to be about the same size. It is best to use the eraser end of a pencil, or a cotton swab, rather than a paintbrush. Dip the cotton swab in paint and dab on your dots.

Mixing Guide:

Yellow + blue =

Blue + red =

Red + yellow =

Yellow + red + a little blue =

3 The leaves on this tree need to be green. Blue and yellow dots grouped together make green. When you come to mix a color, cover the area in the paler color first.

4 Gradually mix your colors until you are happy with your picture. The smaller you do the dots, the better the mixing will look.

GUSTAVE CAILLEBOTTE

Gustave Caillebotte painted in a more realistic way than most other Impressionists. He was interested in photography. Many of his paintings look a little like photographs. He was still an Impressionist, though. He liked to capture fleeting moments in time just like other Impressionists did. In his painting *Paris Street, Rainy Day* below, the three people in the **foreground** look as if they are accidentally wandering through the picture!

CREATE IT!

You will need: old magazines, scissors, glue

1 Make a Caillebotte collage. Find images from magazines. Try to find a street scene, and some closeup photos of people.

2 Cut around your photos of people and put them on your background. Make sure they **overlap** the edges of the picture. Glue them in place.

PAUL CÉZANNE

French Impressionist Paul Cézanne painted many pictures of fruit. He liked to paint solid objects. The pears in his painting, below, look like very solid shapes.

TECHNIQUE TIPS

Cézanne used light and dark shades of thick, green paint to make the pears look very real. He added a dark outline to the shape, too.

CREATE IT!

You will need: a pencil, some pears, pastels or chalks, colored paper

1 Position your pears how you want them on a table. Draw their outline in pencil.

2 Half-shut your eyes and look at your pears. This helps you see where the light and shade is. Using chalks or pastels, add your color. Add some shadows and **highlights**, too.

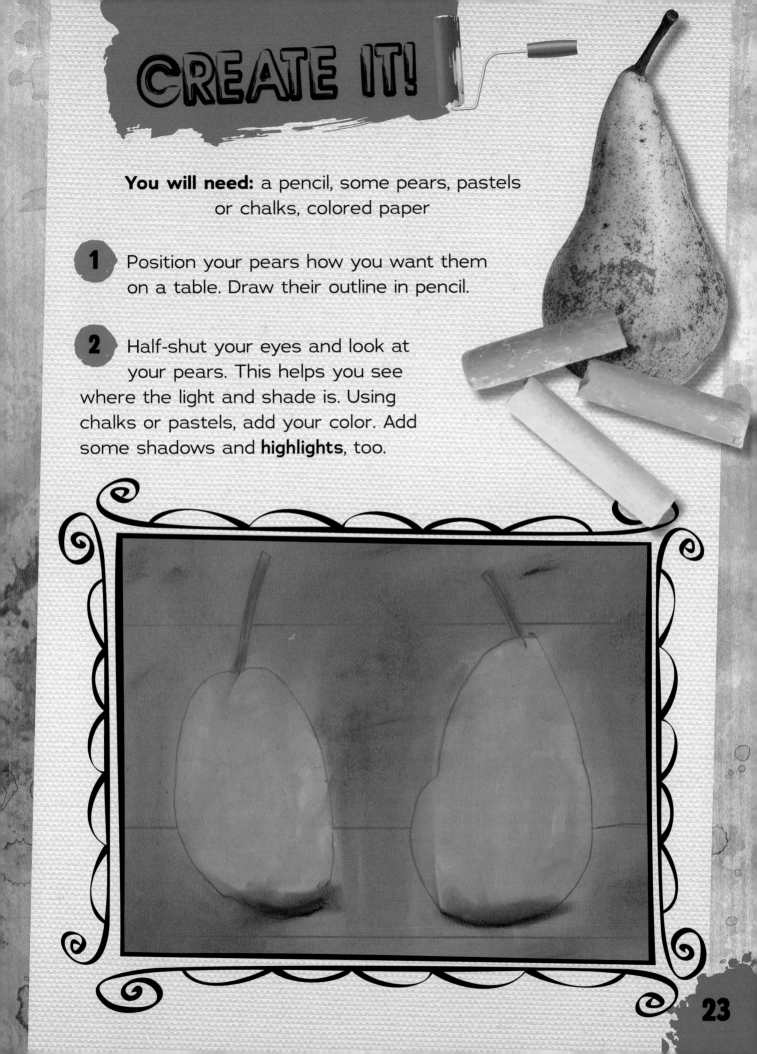

Cézanne's *Still Life with Seven Apples*

TECHNIQUE TIPS

See how Cézanne's brushstrokes went around the apples, helping give them a round shape.

CREATE IT!

You will need: paper, a pencil, thick paint such as poster paint or acrylic paint, a firm paintbrush, some apples

1

First, draw your apples.

2 Using red, yellow and blue, mix up some brown paint for the background. As you paint, keep mixing the colors to make different shades. Add a little white too, if you like.

3 Mix up your colors for your apples in the same way. Add a little more red or green or yellow as you paint. Remember to make your brushstrokes go around the apple.

4 Add a few shadows under your apples.

EDGAR DEGAS

Impressionist Edgar Degas did not like painting outside as many other Impressionists did. Instead, he painted many indoor pictures of ballet dancers and Paris café life. Like other Impressionists, he loved to capture fleeting moments, such as the ballet dancers moving around the stage.

Degas liked to paint ballet dancers from unusual angles. He also liked to paint the effect the stage lights had on their costumes.

Degas' *The Star* was painted from the audience's view above the stage.

CREATE IT!

You will need: a pencil, some scrap paper, colored construction paper, pastels

1 Practice drawing your ballet dancer viewed from above. Do your practice drawings on scrap paper.

2 Once you are happy with your **sketch**, draw your dancer on the colored paper.

3 Color in your dancer using the pastels. Create a colorful background for your picture, too.

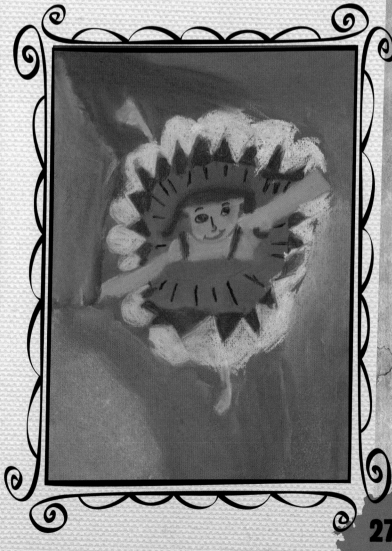

CREATE IT!

Degas created the *The Little Dancer* sculpture below. He used real material for the dancer's **tutu**.

You will need: Wire or pipe cleaners, some colored modeling clay, a piece of tissue paper, an adult to help you

1 Using brown and yellow modeling clay, start to form the head and upper body of your dancer. Save some brown clay for the legs.

2 Make legs out of wire or pipe cleaners. Push them into your model. Ask an adult to help cut the wire, it may be sharp. Cover your model's legs in the remaining brown clay.

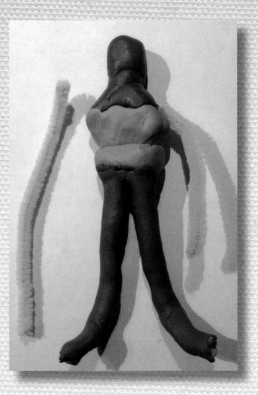

3 Make two wire arms and push them into your model. Join the arms as if they were holding hands.

4 Fold the tissue paper in half to make a long strip. Cut some "v" shapes out of the bottom of the tissue.

5 Fold the tissue into pleats and wrap it around your model. Keep it in place by twisting some wire around it. Now add some clay features to the face.

GLOSSARY

arcs Curved paths.

art critics People who write their opinions about art.

blend To shade into each other.

easel A frame to hold an artist's canvas.

en plein air Painting in the open air.

foreground The part of a scene or picture that is nearest to and in front of the viewer.

highlights The brightest spots in a painting or drawing.

overlap To lie over something and partly cover it.

pointillism Painting using tiny dots of pure colors, which become blended in the viewer's eye.

primary colors Colors from which all other colors may be made. In paint, primary colors are red, yellow, and blue (in light, they are red, green, and blue).

rebelled Fought against authority.

resist To withstand the effect of something.

shades The darkness or lightness of a color.

sketch A rough drawing.

tutu A short skirt that extends out and is worn by a ballerina.

Books

Mayhew, James. *Katie and the Waterlily Pond: A Journey Through Five Magical Monet Masterpieces.* London, UK: Orchard Books, 2015.

Robertson, J. Jean. *A Look at Impressionist Art (Pierre Auguste Renoir, Monet, Degas, Manet) (Art and Music).* Vero Beach, FL: Rourke Educational Media, 2014.

Websites

Ducksters site with information about famous Impressionist painters and their work:
http://www.ducksters.com/history/art/impressionism.php

Tate website with information and links to artists:
http://kids1.tate.org.uk/blog/what-is-impressionism/

Publisher's note to educators and parents:
Our editors have carefully reviewed these websites to ensure that they are suitable for students. Many websites change frequently, however, and we cannot guarantee that a site's future contents will continue to meet our high standards of quality and educational value. Be advised that students should be closely supervised whenever they access the Internet.

INDEX

C

Caillebotte, Gustave 20, 21

Cézanne, Paul 22, 23, 24

collages 21

D

Degas, Edgar 26, 27, 28

I

Impression, Sunrise (Claude Monet) 4

L

Little Dancer, The (Edgar Degas) 28

M

Monet, Claude 4, 5, 6, 8, 9

O

Orchard, The (Camille Pissarro) 12

P

Paris Street, Rainy Day (Gustave Caillebotte) 20

Pissarro, Camille 12, 13

pointillism 16, 17, 18, 19

primary colors 17

S

Seurat, Georges 16

Sisley, Alfred 10

Star, The (Edgar Degas) 26

Still Life with Seven Apples (Paul Cézanne) 24

Sunday Afternoon on the Island of the Grande Jatte, A (Georges Seurat) 16

V

View of Saint-Mammés (Alfred Sisley) 10

W

Water Lilies (Claude Monet) 8